I0467354

Introduction and Overview 2

Chapter 1: Getting started with Social Media **5**

Google email..**5**

Setting up a Gmail account..6

Google YouTube **8**

Setting up a YouTube account 8

Twitter..**9**

Setting up a Twitter account...9

How to personalize your twitter account......................................11

Facebook..**13**

Setting up a Facebook account..13

Getting Started in LINKEDIN...**16**

Setting up a LinkedIn account..16

Getting Started with Pinterest...**19**

Setting up a Pinterest account...19

Getting Started with Tumblr..**21**

Tips for Social media marketing..**24**

Appendix – Accounts information...**26**

Introduction and Overview

Welcome to Step-by-Step Getting Started in Social Media Marketing!

This book is an introduction to social media. It's a crazy world out there online and I wrote this book to help you get started in a few of the most common social media sites. This book is only a starting point... a beginning. Once you have established accounts in the various social media, you'll need to spend time (a lot of time in some cases) to get to know which sites you want to use for your marketing. There are lots of books with lots more details than what you will find in this book. But before you invest in a book that is directed at a single site and how to use it, I suggest you see which sites you like and which you feel will give you the best return on your time invested. The chart below shows the sites that are included in this book and the order in which they are introduced. Also shown are the most popular sites as of September 2014.

I suggest you follow the steps in the book and set up the accounts in the order they appear. Then go back and play around with each site to see which you might want to know more about. At that point, you're on your own...this book can help you get off the ground but to be truly running, you'll need to find a more detailed book (that's what I did, too!).

You will probably find that you will have an affinity to some sites more than others. That's to be expected but if you truly want to engage in social media marketing, then you'll need to focus on the 'biggies': Facebook, Twitter, and LinkedIn. Many social media marketers use only these sites. As time goes on, though, some of the less popular sites will gain more popularity and at that point you may want to add them to your list of sites.

After you've set up these accounts and are using them on a regular basis, don't forget to add the links to them on your website!

I strongly suggest you have a website as well as accounts in social media sites. Remember, every one of the social media sites can, and will, make changes to their sites at any given time. You have no say in the matter. You just need to adjust or drop that social media site. Either way, as long as you have your own website, you do have control of one of your social media marketing avenues as long as you have a website. It is also expected by clients that you have a website. I also suggest that you add links on your website to the various social media that you are engaging in.

In order to keep track of all the accounts you're setting up, I have provided is a chart to capture your account user name, password and any other information in the Appendix. Although it would be great to be able to use the same name for all accounts sometimes you have to get creative with your name because someone else has already used it. Personally, I keep a list of all my accounts on paper as a backup. There are also programs available for this purpose but I like to keep it simple and safe. Not having it on the computer fulfills both for me.

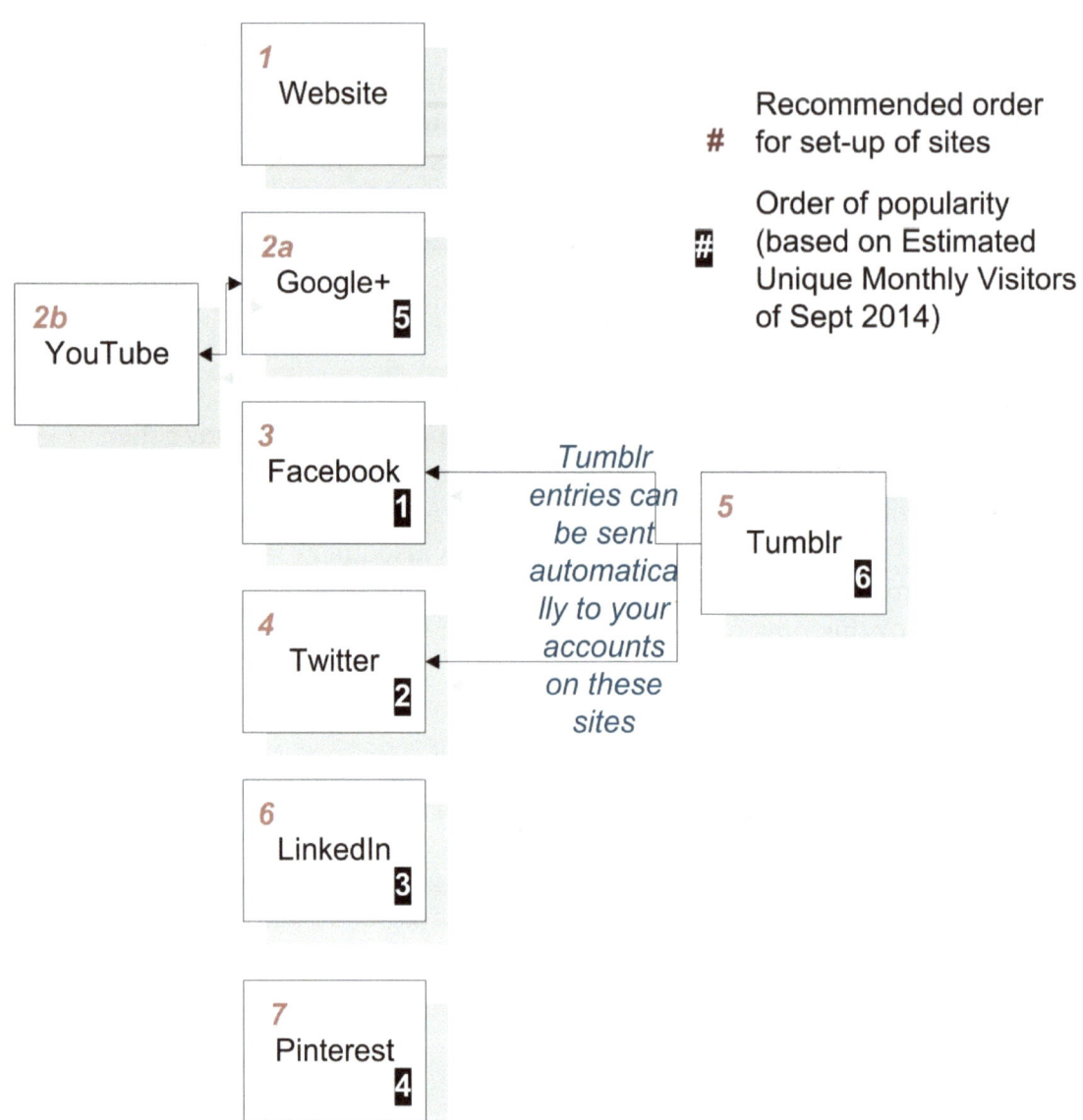

1 Website

Recommended order
for set-up of sites

2a Google+ **5**

2b YouTube

Order of popularity
(based on Estimated
Unique Monthly Visitors as
of Sept 2014)

3 Facebook **1**

Tumblr entries can be sent automatically to your accounts on these sites

5 Tumblr **6**

4 Twitter **2**

6 LinkedIn **3**

7 Pinterest **4**

Instagram **7**	VK **8**	Flicker **9**	Vine **10**	Meetup **11**
Tagged **12**	Ask.fm **13**	Meetme **14**	Classmates **15**	

Chapter 1: Getting started with Social Media

A recommened workflow for social media marekting is to start with a Google account and use it to link all the other accounts when you set them up This allows you to have a single place to go to check your emails from the various sites you have signed up for. This also allows you to create a YouTube account.

IMPORTANT: When you set up accounts with Facebook, Twitter and some other sites, you will want to add an "avatar", which is a visual image that is connected to your business. I choose to use a visual with my website address and phone number, shown below. In some cases I also added my picture. You may want to spend some time figuring out what you want to use an avatar before you get started. If you already have a logo, then use it! If you're not sure what to use, you can leave it blank. Either way, don't spend a ton of time worrying about it but do keep in mind that it provides contitnity with varios social media sites and is yet another way to let folks know who you are.

Google email

WHAT: an email account
WHY: to integrate other social media sites in a single place

NOTE: Keep it 'clean' – no personal stuff!

Setting up a Gmail account

1. Go to Gmail .com

   NOTE: if you already have an account you will need to log out first.

2. Enter the name you want to use (I can be the name of your website or business!)

3. Enter your Username

   NOTE: You may need to reenter until you find a name that is available

4. Enter a password – use mixture of letters and numbers, lower case and upper case

5. Enter your birthday

6. Select your Gender

7. Enter your Phone number if you want, but it is not required

8. Enter your Email address for verification of this new account

9. Enter the captcha

10. Check and agree to terms

11. Go to your other email address (the one you put in on step 9.)

12. Verify the account code

13. Set up profile (will do later)

14. Click Continue on to Gmail

This will be the base of operations for all other social media accounts and Google does a great job with that by automatically putting email in one of three tabs, as you can see in the screen shot below –

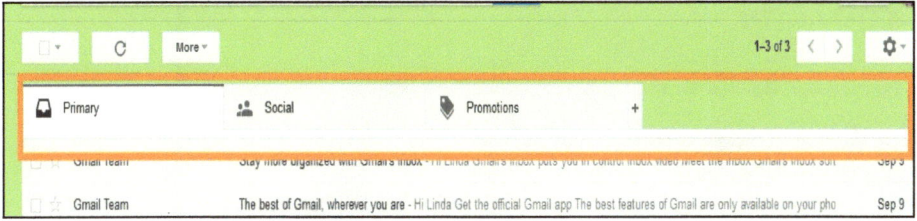

If you now have two Google accounts, you can log on to either one from the main log in page by clicking the **Sign in with different account** link at the bottom of the page, shown below.

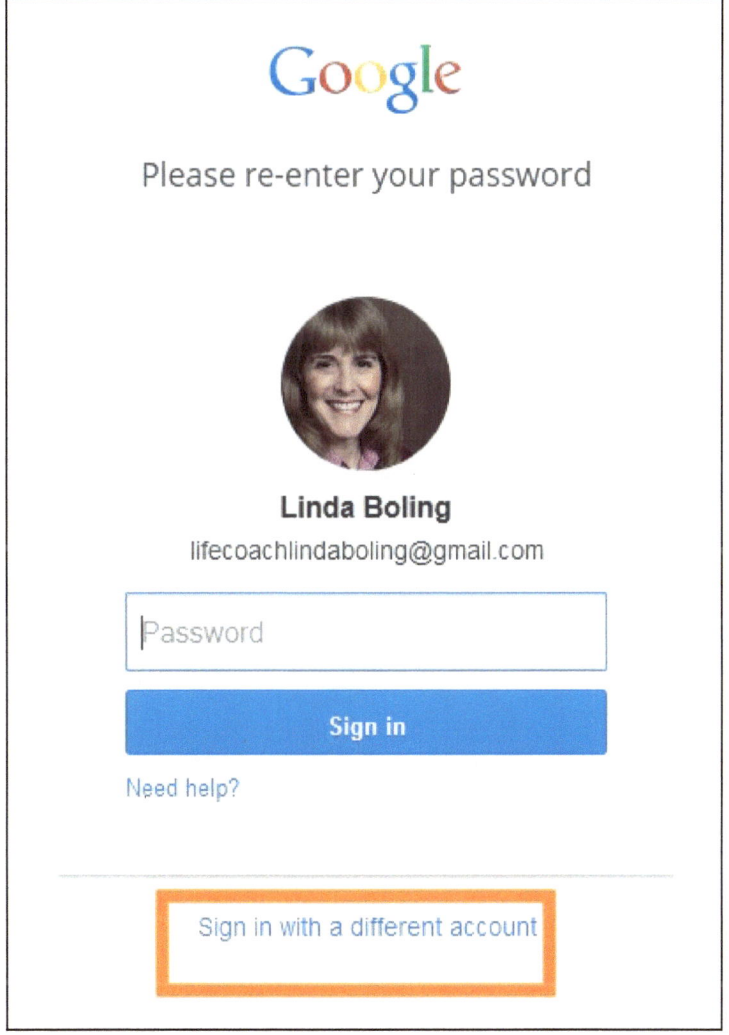

Google YouTube

WHAT: Online videos of any length

WHY: You will want to create online videos as part of your marketing. Also, you can view others to get ideas.

Setting up a YouTube account

YouTube is owned by Google, so once you have gotten your Google account all you need to do is go to YouTube to add an account there.

From your Google account, click the box on the right-hand side and then click YouTube.

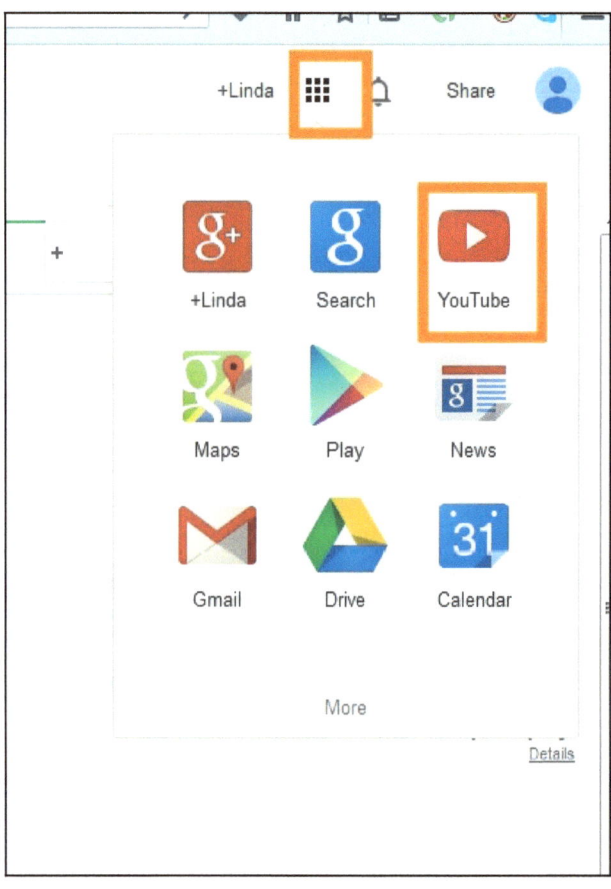

Twitter

WHAT: A 'micro' blog
WHY: It's popular. People go to Twitter to find out what's going on in the world and locally.
What it is: a micro-blog. 140 characters to say what you want to say.
Find what's happening now with people and other that you care about.

Setting up a Twitter account

1. Enter name
2. Enter email (use the google account you just got)

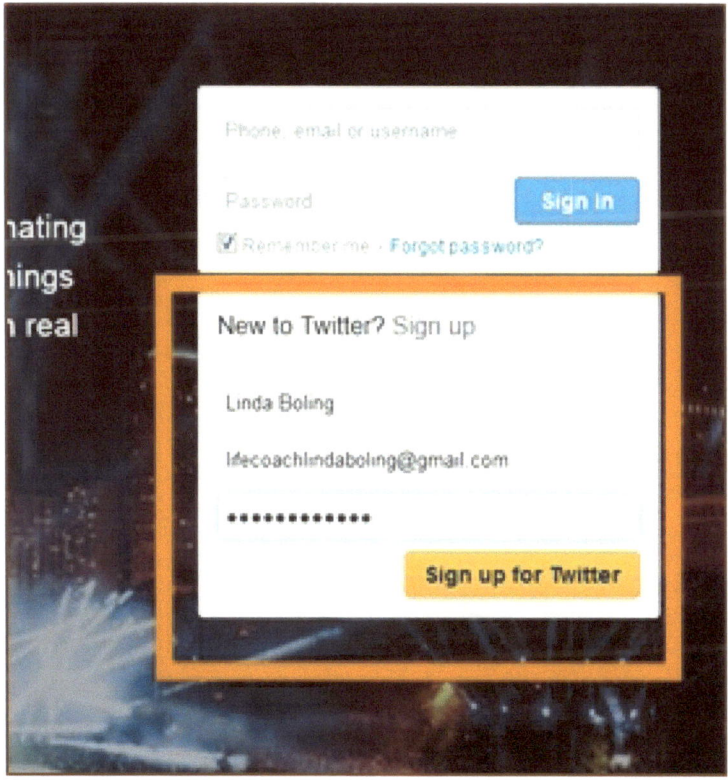

3. Go to your Google account to verify the account. Click on the link in the email.
4. Enter your information in the **Join Twitter today** page.

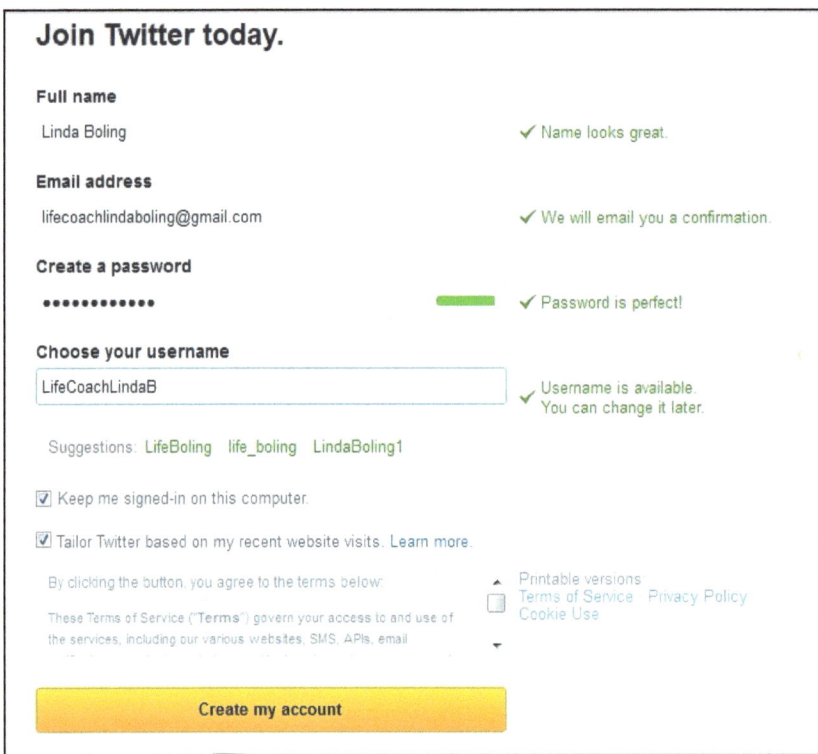

NOTE: When you enter your name, consider using capital's to make it easier to read. For example: instead of lifecoachlinda, I use LifeCoachLinda.

5. Agree to terms of service

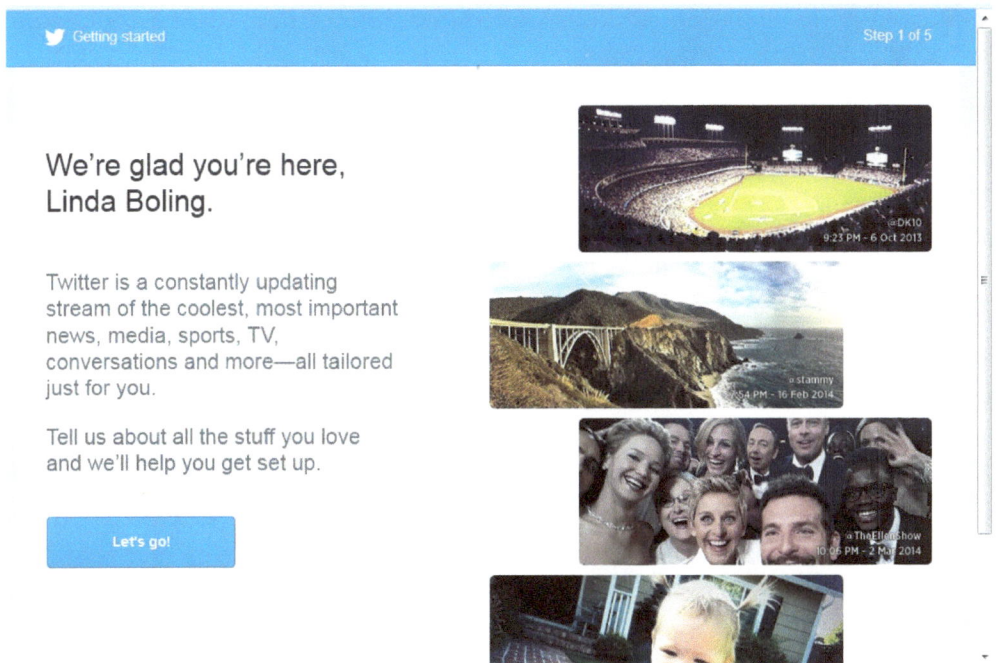

We're glad you're here,
Linda Boling.

Twitter is a constantly updating
stream of the coolest, most important
news, media, sports, TV,
conversations and more—all tailored
just for you.

Tell us about all the stuff you love
and we'll help you get set up.

Let's go!

Now start following… Add things in your industry. Well known people.
Twitter, categories – breaking news, chooses what you are interested in…
TED talks, etc. as you want!

Add some social media feeds such as Tech crunch and Mashable.

How to personalize your twitter account

When you create your twitter account, put it in order right away..
Customize the avatar and background, so you look like you know what
you're doing when other twitter folks see your tweet. This is also part of
your branding!

Click the gear settings and design tab and upload an image for your avatar.
Change the background.

Publish your fist tweet…
You don't need to add contacts at first, just get used to twitter first!

Linda Boling
@LifeCoachLindaB

TWEETS	FOLLOWING	FOLLOWERS
1	39	1

Compose new Tweet..

Who to follow · Refresh · View all

mat honan ✓ @mat ×
+ Follow

KRON 4 News ✓ @kron4ne.. ×
+ Follow

KPIX 5 ✓ @CBSSF ×
+ Follow

Tweets

Linda Boling @LifeCoachLindaB · 19s
@EntMagazine Yep - you just need to get the vision first!
Expand

Neil deGrasse Tyson @neiltyson · 26s
When Queen Elizabeth succeeded King George in 1952, I wonder why the United Kingdom wasn't renamed the United Queendom.
Expand

Retweeted by Mashable
Brian A. Hernandez @BAHjournalist · 1m
Free U2 album announced, launching on iTunes today everywhere. Details: on.mash.to/1nJsVIB #AppleLive

U2

Every iTunes Store customer
119 countries
Available in your iTunes music library
iTunes Radio & Beats Music
Exclusive through October 13

Facebook

Use Facebook if you do nothing else. Even if you "hate" it, remember this is a tool for your business.
If you have a personal account, you can have a single business page. You will still have all functionality without having to create a new account.

Setting up a Facebook account

1. Open Facebook.com
2. Enter your name, Gmail info and a password.
3. Select your Birthday info and sex info.
4. Click Create Page at the bottom of the sign up page

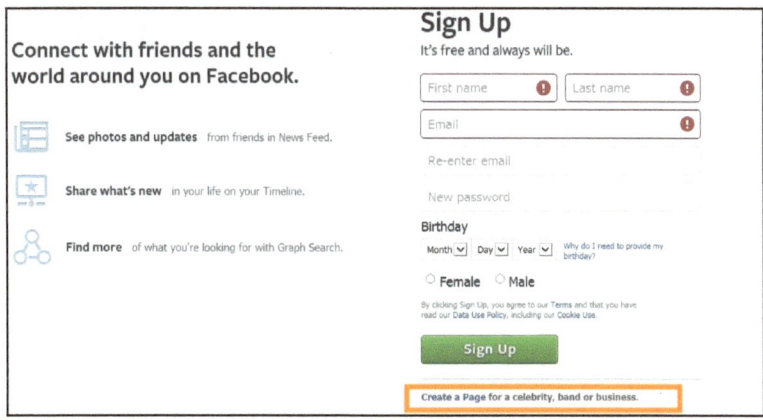

5. Select the type of account.

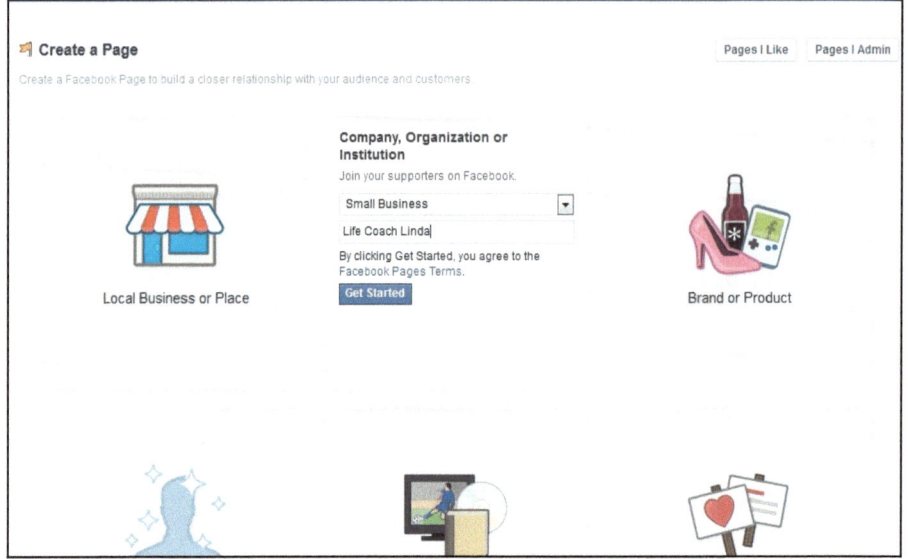

6. Add your business name.
7. Agree with terms.
8. Add your avatar set up page use the avatar for twitter
9. Favorites: stuff on left side … add

You can set up to have all the posts you put in Facebook to also go to Twitter. To do this, you need to:

1. Go to Facebook.com\twitter
2. Click **link to twitter**
3. Authorize app

Everything posted on Facebook will now post to twitter

When authorize things to post… un-check links because you don't want to have to have folks have to click from one link to another. In other words, when you post something in Facebook and then forward it on to twitter, if you don't turn off links then the people will be taken directly to the link sources. If you don't turn off links then they will be taken back to Facebook and then they will have to click on the link there to get to the source of the link.

You can set up all you setting in Facebook by clicking Settings at the top of the page.

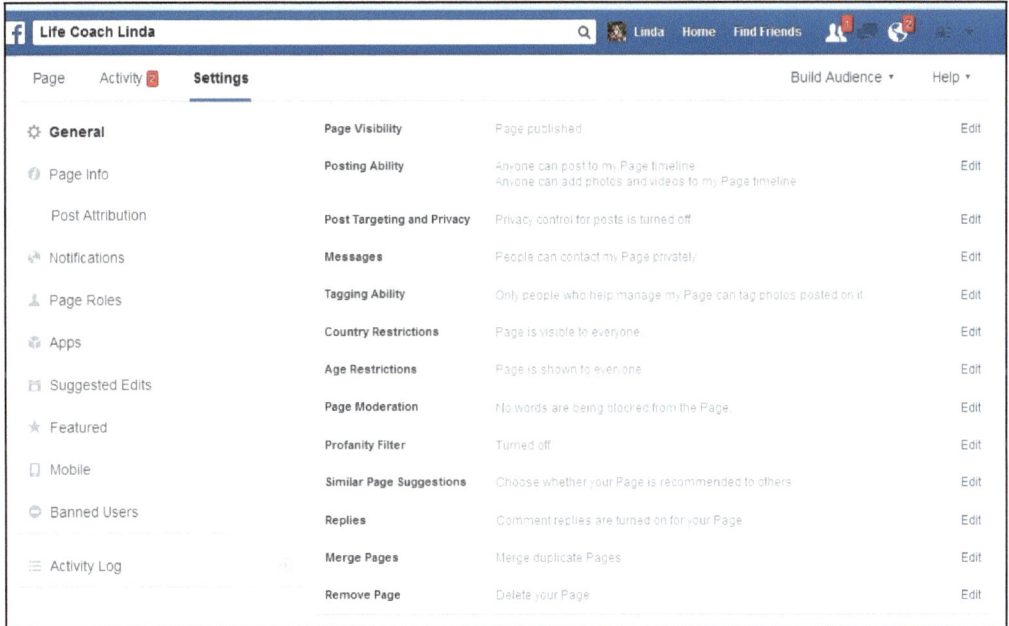

There are a ton of settings. You can take a look at all the possible options and make changes that you want. Generally, folks don't go here so it's important to know what's there and what you can change. Remember that Facebook is always adding new things, so check this page occasionally to see if there is a new feature that you may want to use!

Getting Started in LINKEDIN

WHAT: A professional site that provides overviews of businesses and individuals. It is essentially your resume online.
WHY: Adds credibility to your business

NOTE: LinkedIn is completely different from any other social media in its tone – LinkedIn is formal and business-like. Just keep this in mind when posting.

Setting up a LinkedIn account

1. Go to linkedin.com
2. Enter your first and last name
3. Enter the Google email

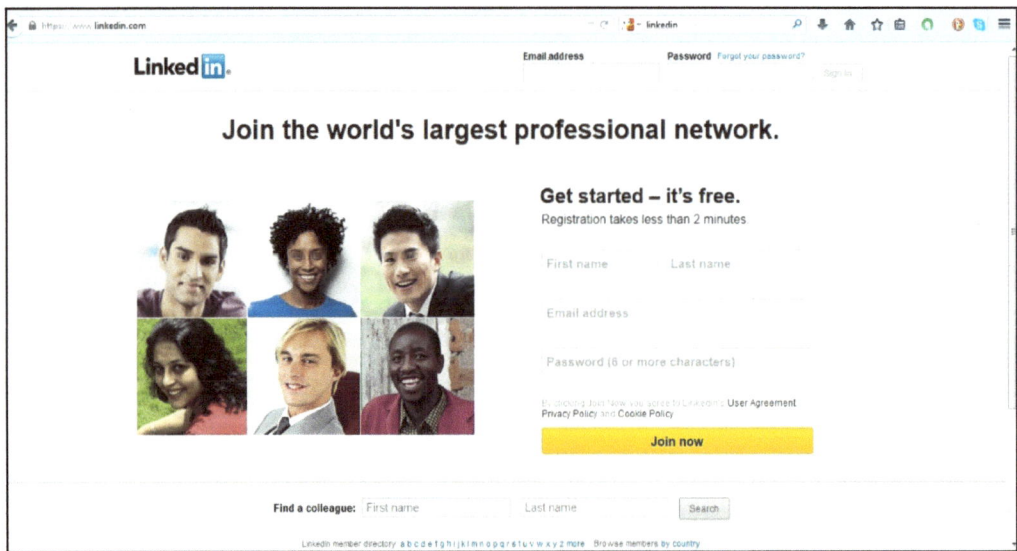

4. Enter a password
5. Click **Join Now**

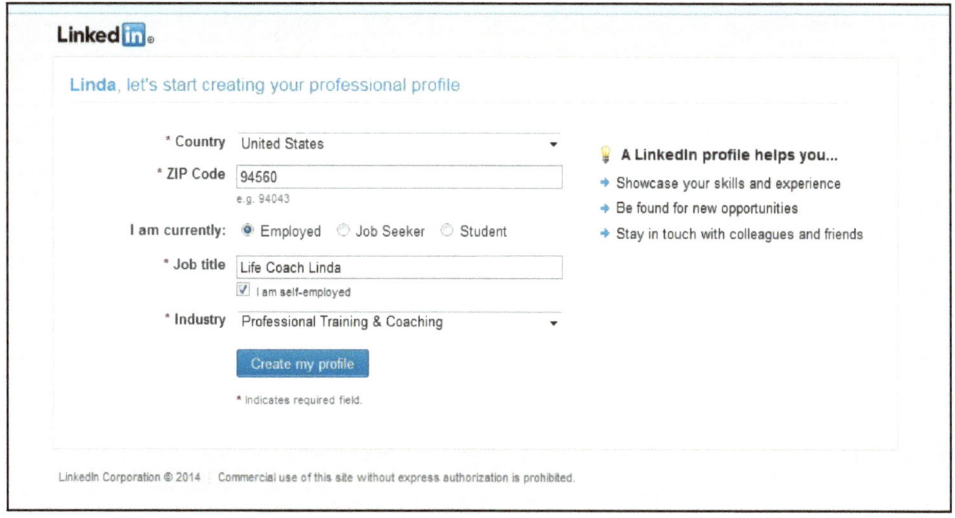

6. Complete the professional profile
7. Click **Continue** if you want to add contacts from your Google Gmail account, otherwise click **Skip this step**.

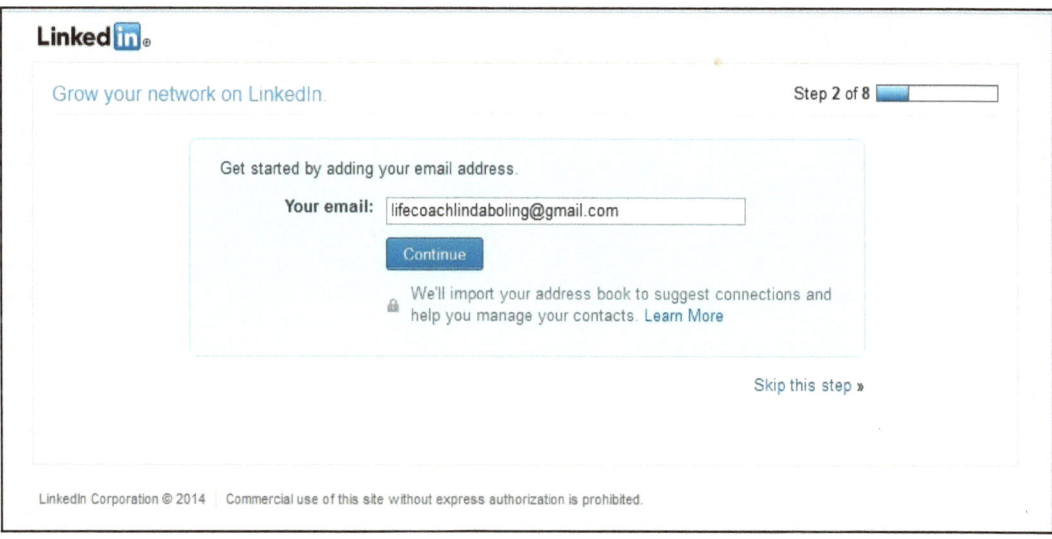

8. Select either the paid account or the free account.

NOTE: You must have premium account for full access to changes and settings. For example, OpenLink is a premium service that allows you to connect with others within LinkedIn via messages. Also, you can have messages sent to your Gmail account as well.

9. Continue entering any information you want to add... you can add a picture, contacts, etc. as it walks you through the set up.

Getting Started with Pinterest

WHAT: A place to capture pictures
WHY: It's very popular with women 25 to 54 years old (And it's really easy to use, so why not!)

Setting up a Pinterest account

1. Go to pinterest.com
2. Enter your user account information

On the main page, you can click your name and a drop-down list of settings.

Check out the user information:
There is a guide to Pinterest at http://www.pinterestguide.com/
Click Your **Business on Pinterest**
Lots of great information for using Pinterest as part of your business!

Hover over name on main page and view boards, setup, etc.

When you're online and see a visual that you like, pin it if you're using the Chrome browser

If you have nice graphics on your website and are willing to share it, you can allow others to PIN IT.
Start a pin board with your stuff and link for site.

NOTE: Always cite your source if you do pin and there is no metadata.

Getting Started with Tumblr

WHAT: A network of specialized blogs that include pictures, videos and other media

WHY: It can be a one-stop place for sending messages to both Facebook and Twitter.

1. Go to www.tumblr.com

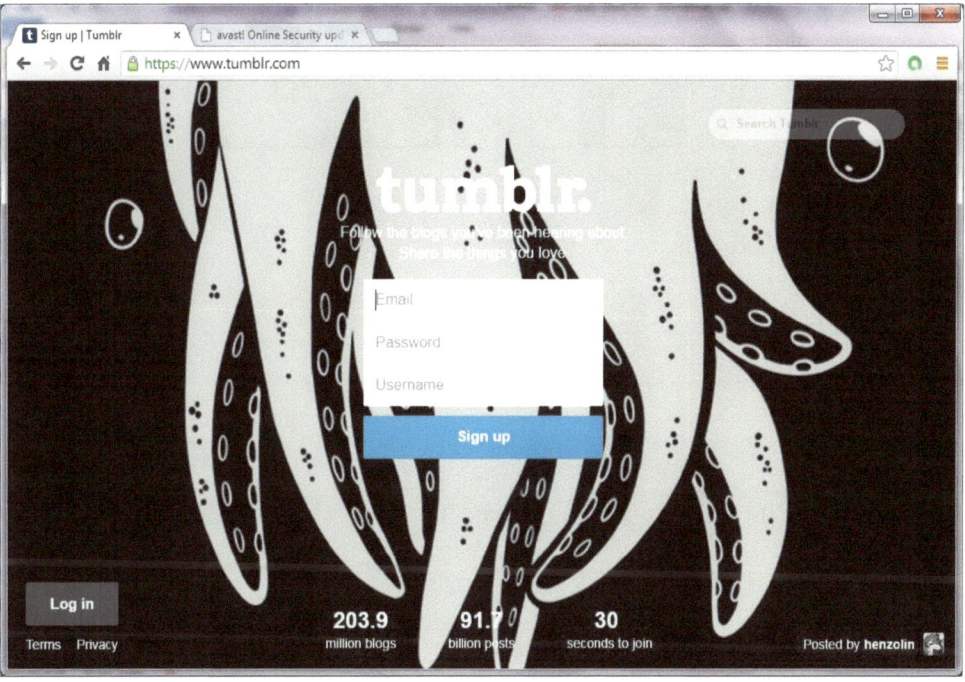

2. Enter your Gmail, password, and user name.
3. Click **Sign Up**.

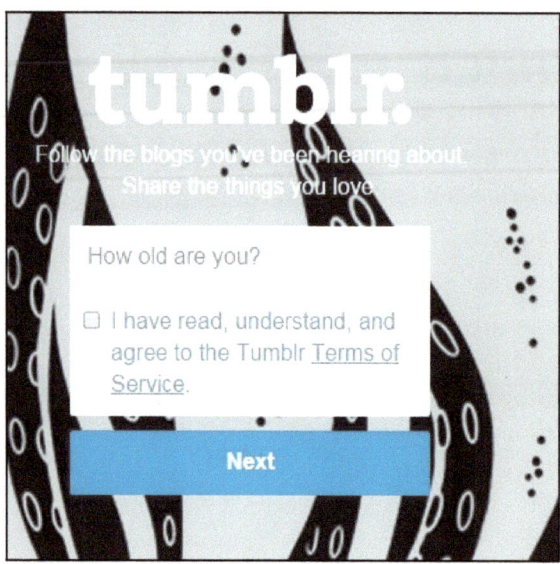

4. Enter your age.
5. Agree with terms.
6. Click **Next**.
7. Enter the captcha.

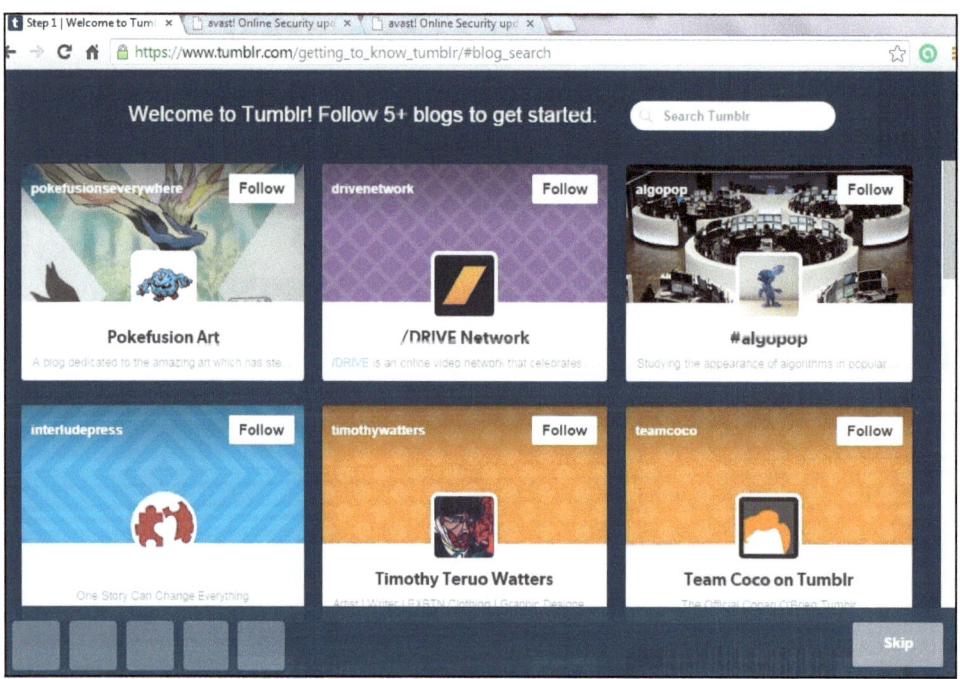

8. **Either choose 5 blogs to follow or click Skip.**
9. Check your Gmail account to validate your account.
10. Click the link in the email.

11. After returning to the Tumblr site, click Continue **to Tumblr**.
12. Choose some blogs to follow. You can use the search box to find them.

At the top of the main page, there are links to help and setting. This is also where you log out.

Settings is where you set up your posts to be sent to Twitter and Facebook.

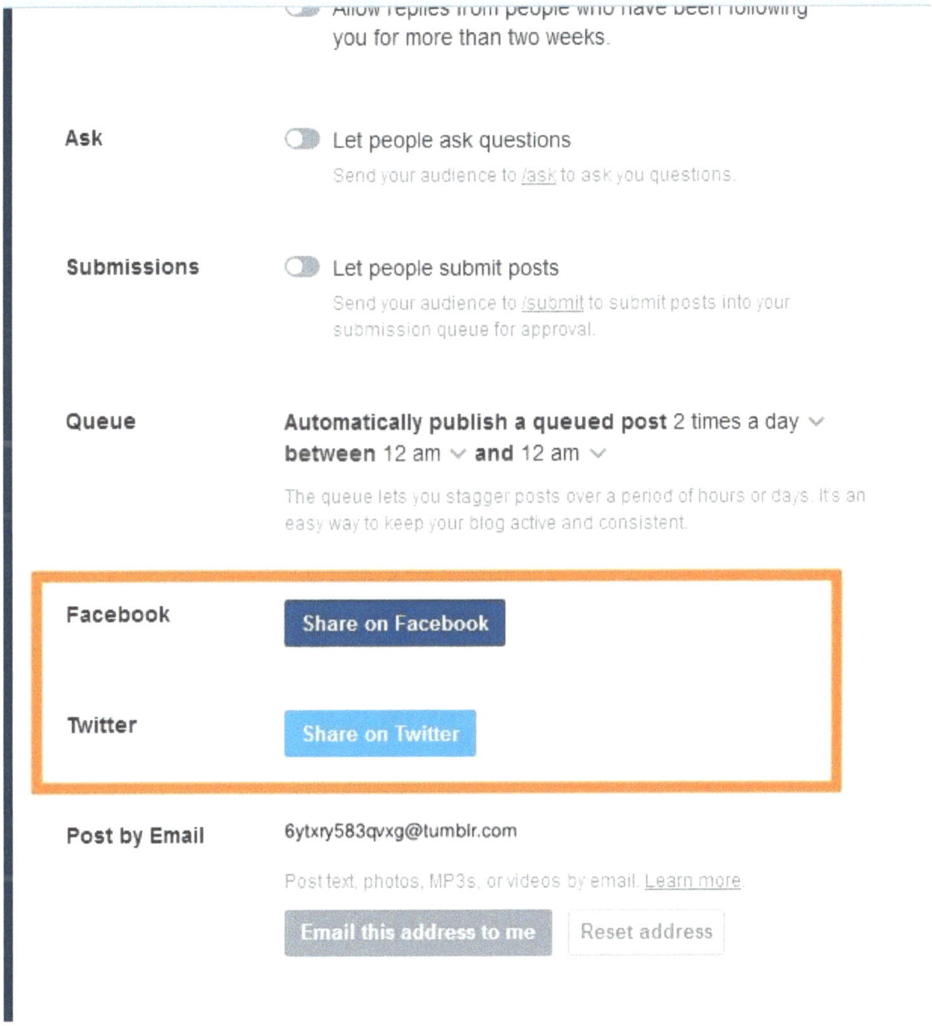

	Allow replies from people who have been following you for more than two weeks.
Ask	Let people ask questions
	Send your audience to /ask to ask you questions.
Submissions	Let people submit posts
	Send your audience to /submit to submit posts into your submission queue for approval.
Queue	**Automatically publish a queued post** 2 times a day ⌄ **between** 12 am ⌄ **and** 12 am ⌄
	The queue lets you stagger posts over a period of hours or days. It's an easy way to keep your blog active and consistent.
Facebook	Share on Facebook
Twitter	Share on Twitter
Post by Email	6ytxry583qvxg@tumblr.com
	Post text, photos, MP3s, or videos by email. Learn more
	Email this address to me Reset address

Tips for Social media marketing

Once you've completed all the set up's you have chosen, you need to spend copious amounts of time with each one to really get a feel for which sites you'll be using for your marketing. If you put an avatar on the sites that allow it, you're already doing some social media marketing! Congratulations!

There are a lot of different views on how to 'do' social media marketing. There are also a lot of similarities. Here are the most common suggestions:

Know what your goal is – why do you need social media? How will it help you meet your goals?

Determine who your audience is and always post to them.

Social media is great for customer service. Make sure that your Contact page on your website is up-to-date.

Posts need to be timely, engaging, and significant to your audience

Create a 'voice' for who you are marketing to – use humor if possible because it will be more likely to be shared with others!

Test different ways of reaching your customers. Try different things and see what works.

Think about what kind of platform you want to use based on what you are sharing – pictures, words, etc. Pick the platforms your audience is using.

Always remember that content IS king. Use stories whenever possible. Tell a story to engage the reader…. It doesn't' have to be a book… the shorter the better.

Use your stories to help the reader/audience get an understanding of the benefits that they will get from your service or product.

Determine how your service or product is different from others that are similar to yours. Find what makes your product or service special and focus on that.

Quality is more important than quantity!

Set up a schedule for yourself to keep up with your social media marketing. For example: Monday, Wednesday & Friday -Facebook and Twitter; Tuesdays and Thursday: other media. Limit yourself to 'X' number of hours so being on the web doesn't distract you from other forms of marketing.

Monitor your competition and yourself! Here's one way:
1. Check their Facebook page – click on **Likes**
2. Check the number of likes versus how many people are talking about it. For example, below this person has 19356 Likes but only 280 people talking about her.

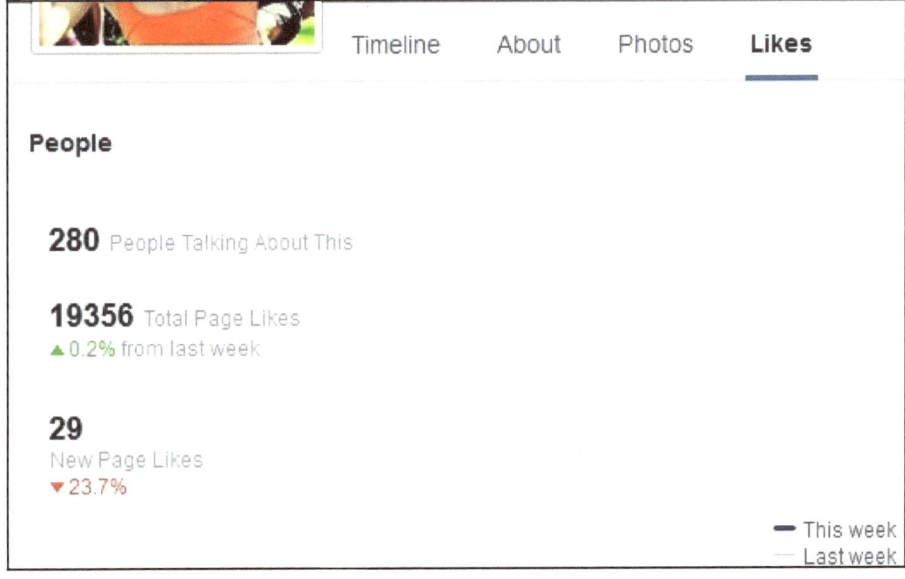

There are lots more to learn! But you're off to a great start... see you online!

Appendix – Accounts information

Account name	Username	Password	Comments (identity questions and answers or other notes)
Google			
Facebook			
Twitter			
Tumblr			
LinkedIn			
Pinterest			

www.ingramcontent.com/pod-product-compliance
Lightning Source LLC
Chambersburg PA
CBHW050428180526
45159CB00005B/2449